Secrets from the Sanctuary

Angela Brown

Dream Gate Publishing

Marietta, Georgia

Dream Gate Publishing
1475 Kolb Lane
Marietta, Georgia 30064
awbrown1@bellsouth.net

Scripture quotations taken from the New King James Version®, Copyright © 1982 by Thomas Nelson, Inc. Used by permission. All rights reserved.

Scripture quotations from The Message. Copyright © by Eugene H. Peterson 2002. Used by permission of NavPress Publishing Group.

Scripture quotations taken from the Amplified® Bible, Copyright © 1954, 1958, 1962, 1964, 1965, 1987 by The Lockman Foundation. Used by permission.

Scripture quotations taken from The Psalms: Poetry on Fire, The Passion Translation®, copyright © 2014. Used by permission of BroadStreet Publishing Group, LLC, Racine, Wisconsin, USA. All rights reserved.

Scripture quotations taken from the Mirror Bible, copyright © 2012 by Francois du Toit. All rights reserved.

Cover Design: G. Claire Brainard
               http://gclaire333.wixsite.com/heartmapping
Book Editing: Angela Brown
Book Layout © 2014 BookDesignTemplates.com

Secrets from the Sanctuary/Angela Brown. -- 1st ed.
ISBN978-0-9970325-2-9

TABLE OF CONTENTS

INTRODUCTION

INTRODUCTION

Do you have a sanctuary? Is there a place you can go to find peace, solitude and refuge from the world around you? Do you even think you need such a place? I believe we were created with a desire and need for a sanctuary that is unique to us. In fact, the Word of God says in 1 Corinthians 6:19 AMP: Do you not know that your body is the temple (the very sanctuary) of the Holy Spirit Who lives within you, Whom you have received [as a Gift] from God?

Being the actual sanctuary of the Living God is truly a sobering thought. Our Father God wants us to realize and accept the fact we were created to be His dwelling place in the earth. Our spirit is where He wants to reside and reflect His image through us. It is His amazing plan for the redemption of mankind.

My husband and I fondly think of our cabin in the mountains of North Georgia as our earthly sanctuary. We can get away from the hustle and bustle of life in our secluded little place in the midst of the National Forest. It is where I have been inspired to write most of the selections in this book.

Actually, it is just a place where I can more easily get in touch with the sanctuary inside myself where Father, Son and Holy Spirit are waiting to communicate with me and reveal Their love, wisdom and revelation. We are blessed to have this cabin and be able to share it with others. But His desire is for each of us learn to retreat to the inner sanctuary of our spirits no matter where we find ourselves positioned on earth.

The Oxford Dictionary of English gives these meanings to the word sanctuary: *refuge or safety from pursuit, persecution, or other danger; a holy place (the inmost recess or holiest part of a temple)*. Wow, that is the place inside our recreated spirit that hosts the fellowship between us and our Living God. Amazing!

As you read through this book, please keep the word "fellowship" in mind. The Father God and Jesus, His Son, have the most perfect fellowship imaginable. Their intent is that you and I enjoy the same kind of fellowship with Them and with our brothers and sisters in the Body of Christ.

God really is intimate. He knows the thoughts and feelings of our hearts even before we recognize them in ourselves. His desire is to share His thoughts and feelings with His sons and daughters. He wants us to know Him intimately. He is eager to share our joys, sorrows and questions and reveal His heart and plans to us daily.

The stories I share in this book are just a sampling of my own fellowship with Father, Son and Holy Spirit. Some of them may sound simple or even childish to you, but they are part of who I am and He doesn't seem to mind. Some of the things I felt God shared with me may not speak to you in the same way they did to me and that is okay.

Our Father can speak the same thing to many people and each one of them will glean something different from His words. That is the beauty of fellowshipping with the Father, Son and Holy Spirit— They are personal and totally unique in Their interactions with each one who wants to spend time listening to Them.

So, I leave you with a thought from the disciple John:

What we have seen and [ourselves] heard, we are also telling you, so that you too may realize and enjoy fellowship as partners and partakers with us. And [this] fellowship that we have [which is a distinguishing mark of Christians] is with the Father and with His Son Jesus

Christ (the Messiah). And we are now writing these things to you so that our joy [in seeing you included] may be full [and your joy may be complete].

1 John 1:3 & 4 AMP

As you read these devotionals, I pray you will be encouraged to retreat to your own sanctuary, enjoy the fellowship of Father, Son and Holy Spirit and receive fresh revelation and awareness of Their sweet affection and desire for a unique intimacy alone with you.

Angela Brown

SPRING

Our Sanctuary

You will show me the path of life; in Your presence is fullness of joy, at Your right hand there are pleasures forevermore. Psalm 16:11 AMP

The Lord has graciously provided us a wonderful retreat in the Blue Ridge Mountains of North Georgia we fondly call our sanctuary. It's just a small cabin on about an acre of land in the middle of National Forestry property. But the naturally majestic surroundings of the forest create the atmosphere of an open-air cathedral. It feels clean here. The air is fresh with the aroma of hemlocks and pines. The Toccoa River gently rolls by at the bottom of the hill. It cools the surroundings, washes down the rocks with transparent torrents gleaming in the sunshine and fills your ears with soothing sounds.

The root Hebrew word for *sanctuary* literally means "a clean place." I feel clean and uncluttered when we come here. As we turn onto the dirt road that winds through the tall trees to our cabin, the anxious confusion and bustle of the city and the weight of responsibilities fade into calmness.

Sometimes I feel like an intruder here because it is so secluded and natural. The few cabins nearby are seldom occupied making the peace and quiet almost deafening. Once I settle into the swing on our screen porch, I become part of the peace that lingers here. My mind automatically turns away from fear, worry and busy distractions. I immediately sense God's presence in this place. I feel such joy here no matter what is going on in my life.

This earthly sanctuary in the woods offers only a small taste of His powerfully majestic and joyful presence. Turning away from the clamor of the world to focus on the Living God is the best way to enter His presence. His presence is the only place to fully experience real joy and genuine peace.

Lord, I pray as I grow closer to You day by day, I will become a consistent participant in Your awesome peace. Your peace passes my understanding, invades my senses and takes me away into the sanctuary of Your heart!

Our Guardian

They will be standing firm like a flourishing tree planted
by God's design, deeply rooted by the brooks of bliss;
bearing fruit in every season of their lives. They are
never dry, never fainting, ever blessed, ever plentiful.
Psalm 1:3 TPT

A stately hemlock tree stands at the front of our property. Our cabin is nestled beneath the shade of its lush green branches. The old tree shows many signs of the years past: broken limbs, gouges carved in the tough bark, a covering of white lichens and green moss.

I have tried to capture its proud dignity on my art paper, but I find it impossible. The branches are so numerous I can't even count them all much less draw them. So, instead, I have just decided to sit on the deck and enjoy the security of its presence.

Even after enduring countless years of strong storms, our guardian hemlock remains stalwart and faithful. Massive roots peek through the mulch floor of our yard for a short distance from the trunk and then disappear under ground. They have supported this giant steadfastly during many seasons of cold and snow, torrential rains and now severe heat and drought. The old tree still stands strong and true even though younger trees nearby have succumbed to the elements.

This scripture from the Psalms describes the life of those "who follow God's ways". They are ones who don't follow after sinners or walk with the wicked. They are ones who meditate on His words constantly and take great pleasure in spending time with Him. Being in the company of Almighty God produces a strength and fruitfulness in our lives that is priceless and timeless.

5

I hope I will remain a faithful guardian of the ground the Lord gives me as well as this stately old tree has guarded the ground we call "our sanctuary."

Lord, grant me grace and power to stand the test of time and the trials of life glorifying your mighty name and displaying your awesome strength. In Jesus' name, amen.

First Surprise of Spring

Delight yourself also in the Lord, and He will give you the desires and secret petitions of your heart.
Psalm 37:4 AMP

My friend and I sat on the deck of our cabin this evening listening to the deep sounds of a hoot owl. In awe, we observed the wonder of God's creation. We reveled in the warm breeze carrying the promise of spring. Wondering when we might see the first hummingbirds arrive, we decided it would probably be a few more weeks when the weather was more consistently warm.

Just as we finished verbalizing our longing for spring's arrival, the familiar hum of our tiny, feathered friend could be heard. Suddenly, I spotted the little bird curiously hovering behind my friend's head. He was just lingering there as if to say, "Here I am, spring is here!"

We laughed in amazement like two little girls discovering a new treasure. We marveled at the Lord's goodness to answer our desires for signs of life and warmth to unfold. We sat for some time into the evening hoping to catch another glimpse or hear another hum of this amazing creature.

Before I went to bed, I joyfully searched our pantry for the hummingbird feeder and filled it to the brim with sweetened water. Out into the crisp, night air I carried the nectar to its designated hanger just outside our breakfast room window. I felt like a child anticipating Christmas morning.

This little encounter with the hummingbird reminds me how the Lord delights in blessing His children with even the simplest of things in life. Nature is always a reminder to me of His amazing provision and creative love toward us.

Lord, thank You for listening to the desires in my heart even when I don't pray them. Help me to always remember Your goodness and sweetness toward me in the simple pleasures of life. I pray for the desires of Your heart to become mine that I might truly delight in You. More than that, keep me ever mindful of Your greatest gift of love in Christ Jesus. In His precious name, amen.

Longings Fulfilled

*For He satisfies the longing soul and fills the hungry
soul with good. Psalm 107:9 AMP*

I awoke early this morning before everyone else.
I brewed a cup of my favorite tea and started a fire to
warm up the room. I began reading an article explaining
the grace of God is the only thing that will bring us His
Spirit in greater measures. Our prayer group has fervent-
ly prayed for this for quite some time. This revelation
encouraged me to continue in well doing and to antici-
pate new measures of His Spirit on the near horizon.

As I put down the article and waited, I began to
yearn for a more tangible experience of His presence and
power in my life. My heart ached for more of Him.
With that thought, I decided to refresh my tea and go to
the breakfast room window overlooking our cabin deck
to watch the sun begin to rise.

As I stood there, I began to pray for another
glimpse of the little hummingbird my friend and I saw
the afternoon before. I wanted one more glimpse before
we left to go home, assuring me that spring was definitely here. I confessed to the Lord it was a childish request,
but it was my heart's desire nonetheless.

Just as I breathed out the last word of my confes-
sion, the winged wonder appeared, lingering at the
feeder enjoying his first taste of nectar for the season. I
stared in great excitement and joy, amazed at the speed
with which my prayer was answered. Wow, if the Lord
would send this little creature to delight my soul so
quickly, surely He will send His Spirit to fill me afresh
with His presence and glory! Thank you Lord for Your
great grace!

Lord, Your presence and glory is worth any wait I must go through to experience You more powerfully and intimately. Thank You for grace to wait cheerfully for Your fullness expressed in the life of Jesus through the power of the Holy Spirit. In Jesus' glorious name, amen.

The Journey of Life

So if the revelation of being a son sets you free from sin,
then become a true son and be unquestionably free!
John 8:36 TPT

As I walked along the soft path strewn with fresh straw from the great pines, the hush of the forest filled my senses. The air was heavy with moisture and the graceful laurels dripped lightly on my head as I passed under their branches. There was an occasional twitter from a hungry bird flitting through the trees looking for a morning snack. The crisp mountain air was filled with the pungent odor of decaying trees that found their last resting place on the woodland floor.

Back and forth, winding down the steep path, dark slithering roots created natural steps that sometimes helped and often hindered my progress deeper into the quiet. But now and again the roar of swiftly rushing life broke the silence and reminded me of the reason for my journey into the great woods. As the droning hum grew louder and louder, a glimpse of white foam could be seen streaking through the trees in perpetual motion.

Suddenly, I stood gazing upward at massive gray walls of granite covered with a veil of white water flowing gracefully downward onto the slick sides of the mountain. The water was effortlessly cascading down the treacherous slopes with unbridled abandon. It didn't hesitate or falter on its course. Each droplet joined hands with another and together they leaped over each precipice crashing onto the rocks below. Their fall was cushioned by the ones that had gone before them making the jagged edges into smooth slides leading to the next jumping place.

The water exhibited no fear or apprehension in its descent. It just flowed together in the force of gravity drawing it downward. I held my breath as I witnessed it plunge into the depths below. I envied its faith and freedom to experience the thrill of destiny.

Lord, grace me to live abandoned, as a true son, to Your leadership and the pull of your call on my life. Amen

Divine Perfection

*...He Who began a good work in you will continue until
the day of Jesus Christ [right up to the time of His re-
turn], developing [that good work] and perfecting and
bringing it to full completion in you.*
Philippians 1:6 AMP

Nature is such a picture of divine perfection.
Whether it is a delightful garden path or a breathtaking
view of the mountains, the natural beauty of growing
things always refreshes and rejuvenates the soul. The
harmony of the plants and trees and sky and waters flow
seamlessly together to present a perfect picture of peace
and power.

But if you take time to look at each individual
plant or tree or flower, you begin to notice little imperfections of shriveled leaves, fading blooms, broken limbs
and even spots of disease that have crept into the plants.
They aren't so perfect as they first appear if viewed as
only parts of the whole.

We are much like those plants with all the little
imperfections of our humanity. We may be shriveled and
weakened by unkind words or the lack of affirmation and
respect. Our youth and vitality might be fading a bit,
making us less attractive and energetic than in days gone
by. We may not be getting the uplifting words of life only God can give, making us hopeless and joyless. Or the
activities of life may have left us broken or diseased in
parts of our souls and bodies.

God created both plants and people in beautiful
perfection, but life in this fallen world is harsh and un-
forgiving at times. However, it seems His plan is to
group us together with others, some very similar to us

and some quite different in appearance and personality. When we come together, allowing space and time for each one to fit in and grow, our beauty seems to be enhanced and our flaws are less noticeable. Together we form a picture of God's perfect creation.

Thank God we were not meant to do life alone. We were created to live with others to help us become better than we are by ourselves. Together, as we walk in love and forgiveness, we can be a beautiful reflection of His perfection and glory. The Body of Christ functions most effectively as we worship and live together in the intimate presence of our Head, Jesus Christ.

Father, keep me mindful of my need to stay connected with others who seek You and know You. Remind me to allow for the imperfections of others as well as my own. Thank You for sending Jesus to redeem us from the results of those flaws and gather us together in the grace and majesty of Your perfect love. In His compassionate name, amen.

Eternal Time

Hour by hour I place my days in your hand...
Psalm 31:15 MSG

For me, mountain time is not another time zone. It is more like another dimension of time. When I sit by the river and watch the water roll by, schedules and appointments are non-existent. Measurements of minutes and hours effortlessly float by with no remorse or care attached to them. In the quiet retreat of nature, I don't worry about getting somewhere on time. I am in the moment. And each moment is a treasure to enjoy without regret or anxiousness. I am present in the moment, not worrying about tomorrow or next month or next year. Time seems to be on my side as I take in the scenery and solitude.

When I am at home in the city, surrounded by phones, TV, computers and calendars, time becomes a task master reminding me that life is short. Things and people and activities are constantly vying for my attention. PRESSURE!

But I don't believe God created us to live in the limits of our time management agendas. I don't recall Jesus being harried and hurried along His way and He only lived a short 30 years on earth. He just listened to the Father, followed His lead and found His way back to the throne room of heaven with all of humanity forever changed by His presence. Wow! I want to live in that time zone.

As I have meditated on these things lately, the Lord has spoken these words to my heart and is changing my perception of time:

"Every moment is precious to Me. I don't waste time—I redeem it. I don't pass the time—I fill it. Time doesn't rule Me—I reign over time.

"Join Me in the rhythm of life as I move through time with bands of light. The light is full of life, building, refreshing and increasing in you and around you. I move with these bands of light through eternity to usher all creation into My presence.

"It's all about bringing creation into unity with Me, into fellowship with Me, into love with Me. I want to love you and experience your presence constantly with no lapses of consciousness. Night takes the body into an inactive state of rest, but your spirit is always awake and active. I am in touch with your spirit continually. There is no time when I am not available to your spirit. You are constantly being empowered to live on earth through My desire.

"Time on earth is temporary, fleeting. Time on earth is measured. Time in My presence is eternal, infinite. There is no time without Me. I AM always. Begin to live outside earth's timetable. Live on eternal time in the eternal purpose of life in My presence."

Lord, I want to live in Your eternal time zone, not pressured by schedules of my own making or the pressure of man's demands. Grace me to flow from minute to minute in synch with Your eternal plan, living out of Your presence and power, just like Jesus did. In His perfect name, amen.

Winds of Change

Come from the four winds, O breath and spirit, and
breathe upon these slain that they may live.
Ezekiel 37:9b AMP

Listen, listen to the winds of change

Blowing in life with freshness and new stability.

Stability not based on schedule or routine,

But on constantly flowing revelation.

Listen, learn, ask questions like a little child.

Your value is not based on your works,

Those works you and others can see.

Your value is far above the works you perform.

Your value is born out of My heart because I like you!

I desire to give you valuable, eternal works,

But let your reward come from our fellowship.

Take joy in the partnering, not in the work itself.

Listen, listen to the winds of change.

Breathe in the stability of new freshness.

Together we will change lives and bring joy to others,

But our real delight will be in our oneness.

Lord, I pray for a childlike heart to just enjoy Your presence. Thank You for breathing new life into me as I focus on Your goodness and You bring change into my life. In the fresh and powerful name of Jesus, amen.

Living Water

*...in a humble (gentle, modest) spirit receive and wel-
come the Word which implanted and rooted [in your
hearts] contains the power to save your souls.*
James 1:21b AMP

As I sit quietly on the porch, I can hear the rushing waters of the river down the hill from our cabin
racing over the rocks toward the lake. The river is ever
moving downward fueled by the force of gravity. As it
rushes through the landscape, everything in its path is
refreshed and restored. Even the water itself is purified
and continually brings life to the surroundings.

As I listen, the Lord speaks to my heart:

"Living water rushes to the lowest point. Living
water rushes to the humbled heart to restore, refresh and
revitalize the dry and thirsty places. Bowing in humility
and repentance draws Living Water from the well of
Life!

"Humility doesn't mean you are low and de-
pressed. It means you acknowledge that I have
something vital to say and you take time to listen. My
words are high and exalted. When you listen and obey,
you move into a higher place. Humility will lift you out
of the mire and into My eternally flowing river of life."

*Lord, thank You for drawing me aside to speak to my
heart. Help me to really listen with a heart to obey and
enjoy Your presence fully. In Jesus name, amen.*

SUMMER

Emerging Life

So above all, guard the affections of your heart, for they
affect all that you are.
Pay attention to the welfare of your innermost being, for
from there flows the wellspring of life.
Proverbs 4:23 TPT

It is another bright and beautiful June day at our cabin. The skies are crystal clear blue. The air is warm, but there is a refreshing, gentle breeze blowing through the trees. What a great day to work outside!

I decided to fertilize the flowers in the pots I have out in the yard and on the deck. The plants are beginning to grow and fill out with a few early blooms to enjoy. We aren't here but a few days a month, so I have to make sure I keep them feed and watered when we come.

We have a large, black iron pot on the deck beside the screen door. I have several varieties of flowers planted in it to attract the hummingbirds we love to watch. As I started sprinkling the fertilizer around the plants, I noticed a clump of leaves, pine needles and moss at the back of the planter. I began to pull at it and quickly realized it was a well-built bird nest with four little speckled eggs inside.

What an amazing and pleasant surprise! I think it's a wren's nest. I have never seen them build one in a flower pot so low to the ground before. They often build in hanging baskets on the wall of my back deck at home. This nest seems so vulnerable being so close to the ground. My hope is that I have not disturbed the nest enough to discourage the mother bird from returning to incubate her eggs.

Truly, new life is fragile. It must be guarded, nurtured and protected. Sometimes it needs to be hidden away until it is able to sustain itself and survive in the harsh elements of nature or the evil of uncaring and selfish souls.

That reminds me of the story of Moses and how his mother hid him amid the bulrushes in a tiny basket so he would not be found by the murdering armies of the Egyptians. She trusted God to protect Moses as she set him adrift in the river. And then, she sent Miriam, her daughter, to watch the little basket to make sure it did not float into troubled waters.

Just like innocent babies need protection from the world around them, our new lives in Christ need to be guarded and protected as well. We must feed our newborn spirits with the milk of God's living word. We must also shield ourselves from distractions and cares of the world that rob us of faith and trust. And we must be accountable to other brothers and sisters in Christ who will help us navigate the treacherous waters of life. Surrounding ourselves with others who trust in God and believe on the mighty name of Jesus will help us to grow, thrive and glow with His own glory and righteousness.

Every new discovery we make concerning God's character and His plan for our lives should be treasured, nurtured in prayer and protected from doubt and unbelief. Then, slowly and surely, we will become strong disciples who can withstand the turmoil of life in a fallen world and become reflections of Jesus to those around us.

Father, thank You for the gift of life in Christ Jesus. Thank You for the gift of Holy Spirit to teach, empower and standby me as I grow up in Your goodness and glory. I pray for You to give me wisdom to recognize the distractions to our life together and to guard this precious faith You have given me. Lead me into relationships with other believers that will nurture and encourage Your life within me. Thank You for Your loving kindness and truth that leads and guides me into Your perfect path for my life. In the mighty, precious name of Jesus, amen.

Divine Paradox

But you are a chosen race, a royal priesthood, a dedicated nation, [God's] own purchased, special people, that you may set forth the wonderful deeds and display the virtues and perfections of Him Who called you out of darkness into His marvelous light.
1 Peter 2:9 AMP

I am sitting on the screen porch of our cabin listening to a gentle rain. Bright sunshine is glistening through the leaves of the trees and casting shadows on the ground. Suddenly, a loud burst of thunder has broken through the quietness like an obnoxious intruder. It seems like a contradiction of weather conditions, but this whole year of weather has seemed that way.

I think times like this are called paradoxes. God's word can seem that way at times--like counting it all joy when we encounter trials! My mind says, "Why would I want to do that?" My mind just wants to whine and complain and look for a quick way out!

But in the midst of the trials come some of the most valuable life lessons we can learn. These lessons can then propel us into greater places of growth and wisdom bringing greater joy to ourselves and often to others. Father God seems to take delight in hiding His treasures in difficult places. He delights in strengthening our spirits through the search. As a result, we can enjoy the true treasure of knowing Him more intimately in the process.

The life the Lord wants to give us is full of this tension between joyful, abundant moments and difficult, demanding moments. I am learning that His perspective is eternally high and mine is temporarily low. Thus, I need an eternal view of life in order to appreciate the temporary place I live in on earth.

Life here is short and fleeting compared with the eternally higher life He is preparing for us as His children. His desire is for us to grow up and join Him in a life of kingdom building. We are learning to live in the Kingdom of Light amidst the kingdom of darkness. That is truly a divine paradox!

Lord, Your ways are mysterious to my mind, but so exhilarating to my spirit. I pray that I would come to trust You more in the paradoxes of Your kingdom. Please, deepen my desire to know You intimately during difficulties as well as triumphs. Increase my desire to live out my destiny as one who lives in Your light in the midst of darkness. In Jesus name, amen.

Sweet Fruit

...I do seek and am eager for the fruit which increases to your credit [the harvest of blessing that is accumulating to your account]. Philippians 4:17 AMP

Down the hill from our cabin a small raspberry patch is growing. We don't know who planted them originally, but last year they produced a very nice crop of sweet, succulent berries. So, we have decided to help them produce more by erecting some trellis for them to grow on.

My husband built sturdy frames for wires to be strung across the patch to support the tall canes. My job was to somehow attach the canes to the wires and get them off the ground. The canes were all bent over and growing into each other making a sticky maze to work through.

We are new at growing raspberries, so we are starting this process a little late in the season. It has proved to be a challenge. The vines are quite unruly and easy to break as I try to attach them to the support wires. There are hundreds of tiny thorns on the canes presenting a real hazard to my fingers. I started out wearing gloves, but they only hindered my ability to secure the canes to the wires. So, barehanded, I gingerly attached each cane to a wire and suffered numerous pricks.

As I painfully worked with the canes and swatted away the pesky gnats, I began to wonder if raspberries were worth all the time, hard labor and injury that we were suffering. Is all this preparation really going to pay off and produce a significant crop of fruit? Only time will answer that question.

But that is the way of faith. We have a vision for something good to come and then we use the resources and strategies we have to prepare a way for the vision to manifest. Sometimes it takes a lot of hard work. Many times we endure annoying and even painful experiences trying to help the vision become reality. Often, we become frustrated when the process takes longer than we expected. Preparing for the crop is not nearly as pleasurable as imagining the harvest and the joy of consuming the fruit.

When the Lord gives us a vision to pursue, I believe He is not so much interested in the end result as He is in our own growth as we prepare to receive the reality of it. If we are wise, we will continually look to Him and listen to Him as we walk out the vision. Those times of watching and listening are the substance of faith and bring the rich reward of knowing more about the God of the vision.

He is the real reward at harvest time. He is worth the inconvenience, the pain and the time spent. The sweetness produced in our lives by working with our God is far superior to that of earthly fruit.

Are the raspberries going to be worth our labors? Maybe. Is knowing God worth our time, energy and pain? Definitely!

Lord, grant me grace to patiently work with You to produce a sweet crop of fruit in my life for your glory and honor and our pleasure. In Jesus name, amen.

Just Be

Do not neglect the gift which is in you, [that special inward endowment] which was directly imparted to you [by the Holy Spirit] ...1 Timothy 4:14 AMP

Today I have spent some time on my deck at home just relaxing and trying to be quiet before the Lord. However, I keep getting interrupted by these tiny creatures buzzing around my head with great speed and agility. Hummingbirds—such fascinating aerialists! They fly about without hesitation, darting up and down and all around seemingly without fear of any kind.

As I began to observe their carefree moves, I realized how simply they live but how brilliantly they display the creative glory of God. They aren't apologetic in their actions, but quite deliberate and bold in their movement. They are very secure in the fact that they are hummingbirds and they just enjoy being hummingbirds. They aren't questioning their purpose or their desires, but they are just being who God created them to be.

You might ask, "Aren't all God's creatures that way?" Well, maybe not. We also have a silly woodpecker that visits the backyard and he occasionally sits himself down on the hummingbird feeder and drinks out of those tiny holes! I think he is having an identity crisis. Isn't he supposed to be pecking on the trees? Actually, he does, but he is not behaving as most woodpeckers do by drinking sugar water out of a hummingbird feeder.

Through all these observations, I have come to the conclusion that many times I act like that silly woodpecker. I have a hard time just being me. I look at others who seem confident and secure in what they are doing, and I begin to think maybe I should be doing the same thing they are. They are really making a display of God's glory by their words and actions. That's wonderful for sure, but the truth is I am not gifted with the same talents. The glory they carry is admirable, but it is actually the glory of the Lord—not their own.

Confidence and security come to those who know who they are created to be in Christ Jesus and accept it with joy and appreciation. The woodpecker may not look as dazzling as the hummingbird as he lives out his life, but those little hummers could never drive a hole into a tree trunk and pull out a bug either. Each has his place in the cycle of life. Without either of them, something vital would be missing.

Our Father has creatively gifted each of us with very specific talents and desires so we can fill a vital place in the building of His kingdom here on earth. As we behold His glory in our daily lives, He can most assuredly convey to our hearts the amazing part we were designed to play as His children on earth.

Lord, thank You for teaching me to just be who I am and do what You have created me to do. Forgive me for comparing myself to others. Help me to see the glory and beauty You have placed in my own life. Help me to display it with freedom and abandonment to the leadership of Your Holy Spirit. Help me to enjoy just being who I am in Christ Jesus. I truly want to soar in the Spirit! In the powerful name of Jesus, amen.

Garden Party

I have come into my garden....Drink, yes, drink abundantly of love, O precious one [for now I know you are mine, irrevocably mine]. Song of Solomon 5:1 AMP

Yesterday I had the joy of attending a garden party at the home of a new friend. She has a lovely home on a wooded lot surrounded by an amazing garden that she has lovingly labored over for many years. Her many varieties of hydrangeas were in full bloom and made a glorious backdrop for the luscious luncheon she served on her patio. We all felt like pampered princesses enjoying a royal feast of food, fellowship and just plain fun.

God's natural creation is a perfect setting for an experience of extravagance. The unique variety of plant and animal life we see in this world is only a taste of the glory and splendor of heaven we can enjoy in the heavenly realm.

Over and above the enjoyment of the natural beauty of God's creative expertise was the joy of sharing the experience with some of my most trusted and dear friends. Our Father God created us to share this life with others who would help us become all we were created to be. And He meant for us to do the same for them and others He might bring into our lives.

Life in God's kingdom is truly rich. I know, for many, opportunities like I just shared are rare if not impossible on this earth. So many in this world suffer unimaginable hardships and disappointments. That is why I am overwhelmed at the goodness I have experienced by the grace of God alone.

My desire is to live with a grateful and appreciative attitude toward my God for the life I have been privileged to live. I also pray He will continue to show me marvelous ways to share His love and provision with others in a way that will open their eyes to His goodness, power and grace available to them.

Life with King Jesus is amazing, thrilling, challenging and overwhelming at times. He pushes us far beyond our comfort zones, but He also meets us there to remind us that He is Almighty and Faithful. The reward of living in His presence here on earth, whether in wealth or poverty, will be an eternal communion in His glorious and loving presence. His love never fails.

Father, how can I thank You for the love and provision you have given me? All I know to do is say thank You and ask for Your continued grace to increase Your life within me and decrease my self-dependence. Make me an offering of your love and faithfulness so others may see Your glory and surrender to Your love. In the precious and powerful name of Jesus, amen!

Brilliance of Butterflies

*For You cause my lamp to be lighted and to shine;
the Lord my God illumines my darkness.*
Psalm 18:28 AMP

In the vast expanse of the forest, under the canopy of towering evergreens and oaks, there is a surprisingly delicate creature that flutters its way freely through the undergrowth of wildflowers and blooming shrubs. The butterfly is certainly a surprise to me every time I enter the woods. A cottage garden seems to be a more familiar and sensible setting for this dainty winged wonder. Amazingly, it appears to be at home in either place.

On one particular excursion through the forest, I noticed a large black Monarch pleasantly perched on the tiny white blossom of a wildflower alongside the dirt road. It never seemed to notice me bowing closer to get a better glimpse of its marvelous composition. It nonchalantly perused the minute blooms for tastes of sweet nectars and gracefully raised and lowered delicate wings as if caught in a slow motion replay.

Gazing on the intricacy of its wing structure, I was captured by the vividly distinct blue dots decorating each one. They seemed to form a perfectly planned pattern brilliantly accented by a velvety black background. The pattern was surrounded with a thin strand of gold. It was like a masterful piece of art with the ability to fly!

Pondering this masterpiece as I continued my walk, I began to think of the blue dots and how they were contrasted against the dark wing. It seems that sometimes in our darkest moments in life, we can actually be blessed with our most brilliant revelations. These tidbits of wisdom can stand out like a beacon to brighten our outlook and strengthen our steps. And if we pay close attention to them, they will form a pattern guiding us through the darkness, helping us see the treasures hidden there.

Strands of gold are threaded throughout each dark night of the soul in order to form a tapestry of priceless knowledge and wisdom. Only the free spirit can wear this creation and go about life displaying the glory of their Creator while tirelessly searching for sweetness even beside a dirty road.

Open my eyes, Lord, to see the valuable treasures of Your wisdom and strength when life seems to get dark. I want to be able to enjoy Your sweetness in every experience. Trusting in Your goodness, in Jesus' name, amen.

The Aroma of Life

*Because of Christ, we give off a sweet scent rising to
God, which is recognized by those on the way of
salvation--an aroma redolent with life.*
2 Corinthians 2:15-16 MSG

Fresh herbs are so delightful to have in your garden. Their taste and aromas fill your senses with pungent flavors and delicious fragrances. Sadly, I have only a little success growing a few varieties on our back deck in flower boxes.

However, my husband, the master gardener of the family, is able to produce a bumper crop of vegetables in our small garden plot beside the driveway. In the corner of his tomato bed, a very large rosemary bush thrives year after year. It is one of my favorite herbs to use as I cook. I love to cut a few extra sprigs just to put in a glass of water in our kitchen. The scent is so refreshing and the tender green leaves offer a delicious accent to our foods.

That rosemary bush just amazes me. It sits out in the hot sunshine of summer with little or no shade at all. Of course, it gets the benefits of living in the corner of the master gardener's tomato bed. But in the winter months, it gets no attention at all. The harsh, cold winds blow on it and it has no shelter from storms or frigid temperatures. Nevertheless, it continues to spread out and grow new branches every year. My husband even has to prune one side of it back during the growing season just to get through the garden gate. It stays green all year long and produces enough to share with many of our friends and family.

The Lord, our master gardener, also lovingly tends to our needs throughout all sorts of circumstances. He waters us with His words, both those in the Bible and those He speaks to our spirits if we stay still long enough to hear. He prunes our unruly growth so we can compliment others, not overpower them. He allows the good and joyful as well as the harsh and difficult circumstances of life to help us put down deep roots sustaining us for many seasons. He is not a negligent and distant gardener, but a tender and wise keeper of life.

His diligent management of the ones who choose to linger in His intimate presence and submit to the pruning process always produces a bumper crop of sturdy lives. Those lives continue to put out tender shoots of pleasant, fragrant and life-giving growth, nourishing and refreshing others. It is a good thing to be a plant in the Master's garden.

Lord, help me to remember, even in the harshest circumstances of life, You are there nourishing, sustaining and empowering me to thrive. Help me to quietly linger and listen in Your sweet presence. Thank You for Your tender and wise care making my life a sweet and life-giving aroma for others to experience Your glory. In Jesus name, amen.

Down by the Riverside

*In returning [to Me] and resting [in Me] you shall be
saved; in quietness and in [trusting] confidence shall be
your strength. Jeremiah 6:16 AMP*

Sitting by the riverside is a heavenly place to
spend the afternoon. Time drifts by as quickly as the
water rushes over the rocks past the lush green foliage of
the trees strewn along the banks. You can get lost here
at the river's edge.

The melody of birds singing and insects buzzing
coupled with the low hum of rushing water creates a
symphony of peace and serenity. There is an intricate
mix of force from the river's current, the delicate wildflowers growing on the banks and majestic trees in the
forest. It is awesome beyond words!

Again, I try to capture the scene with my amateur
art skills and quickly become frustrated. Instead, I begin
to ponder the idea that this must be a bit like heaven at
the foot of God's throne: watching the force of the River
of Life pouring forth from beneath His royal chair and
seeing the brilliant rainbow of colors surrounding His
presence. Picturing the peaceful gaze of love and ac-
ceptance in His eyes is too much for my imagination to
recreate, but there is a great longing to actually experience it.

His love, power and majesty are truly awesome
as they flow together to form a place of rest. In His rest
you can come and lay down your worries and confusion
and learn to relax. At the foot of the mighty Throne of
Grace, time is endless and you can get lost in the One
who holds all of creation in His hands.

Thank You, Lord, for a touch of heaven down here by the riverside! But help me, Lord, to experience Your heavenly touch no matter where I am. Teach me how to really rest in Your presence and hide in You and Your peace. In Jesus name, amen.

Voices of the Streams

Set your gaze on the path before you. With fixed purpose, looking straight ahead, ignore life's distractions. Watch where you're going! Stick to the path of truth, and the road will be safe and smooth before you.
Proverbs 4:25-26 TPT

This morning I walked out the road from our cabin before the cool air gave way to the noonday heat of August. After huffing up our steep hill, I finally reached a more level place in the road. Briskly I began to wind my way through the National Forest Reserve. This walk is so relaxing and pleasant. The only sounds are the rustle of leaves on the giant hardwoods and the chirping of birds swooping through the branches.

Along the way there is an enchanted little valley covered with lush green wild rhododendrons and mammoth hemlock trees. The foliage is so thick you can barely see the brilliant blue sky. The gravel road becomes almost like a creek bed from the moisture of two streams sliding down the mountain and crossing under the road. It is a sheltered and secluded respite from the heat of the day.

As I paused between the two streams to enjoy the cool peace of the valley, I closed my eyes to listen to the sounds of the forest. Adding to the gentle noise of blissful breezes and twittering birds was the gentle trickle of water making its way over and around the massive collection of smooth rocks covering the valley floor. The drought of summer had slowed down the pace of the streams considerably, but there was still enough water flow to stir up a thirst in my mouth.

I never considered the many tones of water before. One of the streams comes down toward the road on a fairly level and straight path. The water evokes a sense of tranquility as it slowly trickles through the rocks. These peace filled sounds are easily associated with the quiet of the forest.

But besides the tranquil tones, I could hear another sound much louder and more demanding of my attention. It came from the other stream precariously winding its way through the forest down a steeper slope of larger boulders. This water moves considerably faster making a greater impact on the rocks as it speeds downward.

The first stream took a path of minor resistance and peacefully meandered its way toward the river below. The second stream chose a more adventurous path on its journey loudly declaring its intention all the way down the mountainside. Both streams will eventually reach the river below, but with distinctively different voices.

These streams remind me of the choices we have to make in our lives. Many people choose the path of least resistance going about their daily lives. Most of the time it is a more peaceful path with fewer surprises. They can almost go undetected among others along the way. They are probably not sure of where they are going or even if they have arrived. Nonetheless, they don't have to move too fast or go out of their way to get where they're going. They just meander along without much fuss and very little impact. Their way seems to be a safe way to travel. However, somewhere along the way when the path gets level, they might stop moving and disappear underground like a quiet stream.

On the contrary, others choose to follow a path like the second stream carrying them downward at a much faster pace. Again and again they may face many large obstacles causing them to adjust their direction around seemingly insurmountable odds. The extreme conditions of the pathway require them to continually declare their intent and to focus on the goal of reaching the river. They must constantly move downward to a lower elevation in order to move more quickly along the way. If they get distracted with the scenery around them, they could miss a step and waste valuable time or even crash.

This path is not a silent one, but requires a louder voice shouting in advance, "I'm coming through!" Progress is more notable and the impact of decent can cause a lot of interruption in the lives of those around them. It can actually change the landscape they move through! Many will know they have been that way and their footsteps can be easily traced.

Many say the second path is too hard and dangerous. It is too presumptuous and bold. It produces too many chances for error and disapproval. To follow this path, one must be full of adventure, vision and, most of all, courage. It is an all or nothing lifestyle and the reward can be glorious even though treacherous.

The more level and straighter path is certainly less precarious and appears to be simpler and less confusing requiring very little voice at all. The snail like pace can create more opportunities to get lost in the surroundings and forget the goal. If the path becomes too level, progress can come to a complete halt and the journey is over quickly. The peace can fade into boredom and the goal is ultimately dismissed. And even though this path seems safer in the beginning, the chance of success decreases with each listless step.

The voice of peaceful water is certainly refreshing to my soul for a time, but this newly discovered, bubbling, churning voice of courage takes my breath away and excites my spirit within. I sense it stirring in me the need for adventure and the desire to move downward toward the expanse of the free flowing river and the promise of life it holds.

Ultimately, I pray I can be a voice of peace in the storm and a voice of courage to the weary, bored and lost. There is a time and place for each voice to have its say and finish the journey together in harmonious tones of oneness.

Lord, I ask for a heart of courage to impact the landscape around me for our glory. Keep my heart and mind focused as I follow You down the path You want me to travel. In Jesus name, amen.

FALL

Changing Seasons

And let us not be weary in well doing: for in due season
we shall reap, if we faint not.
Galatians 6:9 KJV

Harvest time is here. The celebrations are beginning. The bounty of summer is being gathered, and the hint of autumn is in the air. The dogwood leaves are laced with red, and berries are appearing in their clusters. Late summer blooms are changing from pale hues of pinks and blues, to richer shades of yellow, orange and red.

Bushels of apples and baskets of gourds line the storefronts. Acres of pumpkins and bales of hay dot the landscape heralding the diligent labor of a long, hot summer and announcing the coming of autumns' abundance.

Schools, churches and villages across the countryside complete their fall festival preparations in joyous anticipation of the harvest at hand. Instruments of celebration are being polished and tuned to fill the atmosphere with the newest sounds of praise and rejoicing.

Each season closes its door with sounds and sights teaching us valuable lessons to prepare us for the next season on the horizon. The smaller yield in our crops this year is a reminder of the lingering bite of winter diminishing the bloom of spring and decreasing the harvest of fall.

For some there is a hint of sadness as the lazy days of summer pass into shorter daylight hours filled with the labor of the harvest. For others there is great anticipation of cooler, crisper days and clear, refreshing evenings to rest from the heat and dryness of the past season.

But for all who are attentive to the changing times, there is a growing hope for the future hinting of peace on earth and goodwill toward men. With each passing of time, there is wisdom to be gleaned for the days ahead and promise for the coming challenges.

Wisdom has come to give us rest from our labors, prepare us for the promise, strengthen us for the work and ready us for the glorious harvest ahead. It's time to dust off the dirt of the long, hot summer, put on our dancing shoes, pick up our instruments and clear our throat for new songs to be sung!

Lord, help me fully appreciate the different seasons of my life. Help me look for the wisdom from each past season and apply it to the present one. I want to take hold of oneness with You as a valuable gift to treasure always. In the precious name of Jesus, amen.

Brief Encounters

Look carefully then how you walk! Live purposefully and worthily and accurately, not as the unwise and witless, but as wise (sensible, intelligent people), making the very most of the time [buying up each opportunity], because the days are evil. Ephesians 5:15-16 AMP

I woke before dawn this morning and ventured outside hoping to catch a glimpse of a meteor shower. The sky was clear and the stars were brilliant in the cool, crisp air. Usually you have to wait a few minutes for your eyes to adjust to the darkness to see many of those rare twinkling lights. But only a few seconds passed when I caught sight of the streaking trail of a tiny meteor.

Whoa! It almost took my breath away as it appeared and disappeared so quickly. How amazing they are! How swift and fleeting was the moment of recognition! I stood there quietly gazing into the darkness holding my breath, hoping to see another flash of light speed into nothingness. But, alas, the show was over for me. I started getting cold and gave up the quest.

As I thought on the brief meteor drip (certainly not a shower), I was a bit disturbed. How brief some events are! How rare some moments are! Life is full of these brief, rare events that can dazzle and astound us in our every day lives. Unfortunately, I think we miss quite a few of these precious moments of interruption in our scheduled routines.

I felt the Lord nudging me a bit, making me wonder how many rare events have come and gone without me taking time to gaze into and enjoy their wonder. When a chance meeting or a unique opportunity comes my way, am I so caught up in the routine, scheduled activities that I am missing His delightful displays of wonder and amazement sent to enrich my life?

Am I missing an opportunity to spice up my relationship with Him or another person? Am I ignoring chances to enrich another with a spontaneous gesture or word of encouragement? Some of these fleeting moments could paint a picture in a heart lasting a lifetime and changing the course of a dead end path.

Miracles don't happen every day--or don't they? Now, I am beginning to think some of God's miracles are going unnoticed and unappreciated in my life. I may be missing out on some pretty amazing opportunities to brighten up the world around me with a streak of twinkling light that takes the breath away! Oh my, I think I need to pay closer attention! How about you?

Lord, thank You for brief encounters with Your goodness and generosity towards me. Forgive my dullness and insensitivity to Your fleeting opportunities to be blessed and to be a blessing to others. I ask for Your help to be more attentive to Your Spirit and the unexpected blessings of interruption in my daily routine. Thank You for Your constant displays of love throughout the day. In Jesus name, amen.

The Twisted Maple

He who discovers the poetry of truth, faces the light
unashamedly-his lifestyle boldly displays the workman-
ship of union with God! His works speak for themselves -
"Made in heaven - wrought in God!"
John 3:21 Mirror Bible

Walking along the riverbank today, I discovered a strange looking tree. It was a maple. I hardly recognized it because of its distorted shape. The trunk of the tree was fairly large for a maple tree and it was quite bent and twisted. It reminded me of a wet towel twisted over and over in order to squeeze out all the water.

For years this maple tree has searched diligently for light amidst the larger evergreen trees surrounding it. Year after year as it grew, the quest for life giving light required it to contort itself to find a spot to bask in the warmth of the sun. Time and again, the necessity for light created a persevering power in this tree to survive even though surrounded by darkness.

Each spring new green leaves appear to add to the shade of the dense evergreen woods. Every fall the exquisitely shaped leaves turn into brilliant offerings of red and gold causing it to shine out among its giant hemlock neighbors. Even as the glory of fall begins to fade, the maple's droppings brighten the forest floor and float down the river like small vessels at sea.

I so admire and appreciate the way this valiant tree has displayed the spirit of its Creator with such amazing dignity and fortitude. What a display of diligence and passion for light and for life!

Lord, grant me grace and tenacity to come out of every dark place in my life and seek Your life giving light. In the powerful name of Jesus, amen.

Reflections

...In gazing with wonder at the loveliness of God displayed in human form, we suddenly realize that we are looking into a mirror, where every feature of his image articulated in Christ is reflected with us! The Spirit of the Lord engineers this radical transformation; we are led from an inferior mind-set to the revealed endorsement of our authentic identity.
2 Corinthians 3:18 Mirror Bible

Recently, my husband and I had the pleasure of visiting dear friends in upper Michigan. We had a few days together at their cabin situated by a beautiful natural lake in the midst of a secluded forest. The trees were just beginning to show some autumn color. Only a few had become brilliantly bold with reds and yellows.

One still, crisp morning we took a kayak ride on the lake. The water was as slick as glass. As we slipped silently through the water, our paddles created gentle ripples across the face of the water. We decided to stop in a small cove and take in the quiet beauty surrounding us.

As we sat there the water became like a huge mirror reflecting the glory of the trees bordering the lake. The colors were only slightly different in the reflections as they were on the trees themselves. You could even see the wispy clouds floating through the brilliant blue skies. It was so serene and majestic. You could have taken a picture of the reflection and passed it off as the real thing. It was captivating. I could have spent the whole day just floating and watching the reflections in the water.

The day before there was a breeze blowing and I noticed the reflections, but they were a bit distorted. The colors were the same, but the images of the trees were fuzzy and not as distinct. You could tell they were trees and their motions were the same, but the reflections were not as clear and serene.

As I have pondered those moments on the lake, it seems we are much like the reflections of those trees in the water. As we gaze on the Lord in His majesty and follow His teachings, we begin to reflect His glory and splendor in our lives. Others begin to notice the similarities of character and behavior. And when we are really gazing and meditating on Him, others will want to gaze at us and wonder at what they see.

Life is not always serene. The winds come and blow like intruders making ripples in our lives and distorting the image of the Lord in us. The Lord comforted me with this thought: If we continue to behold Him in His Word and trust in Him, we will still reflect the colors of His glory as we wait for the disturbances to pass. In fact, our gazing and obedience can even usher in the peace and quiet helping us to reflect a truer image of the glorious One who loves us so!

Lord, thank You for encouraging me with these images of Your glory. Thank You for giving us Your Living Word to lead us, inspire us, comfort us and direct us when the winds blow and turmoil disturbs the waters. Thank You for making me into a true reflection of Your glory as I continue to gaze on Your splendor and majesty. In the mighty, strong name of Jesus, amen.

Delicious Daybreak

...His [tender] compassions fail not.
They are new every morning;
great and abundant is Your stability and faithfulness.
Lamentations 3:22-23 AMP

Ahhh! Cool, crisp air!

Golden hues highlighting the dark sky,

Faint chirping of early birds,

Gentle hum of clean water on river rocks.

Smokey gray mist creeps through the trees.

Evergreen aromas permeate breath.

Timid deer graze on moist grass while

Bold black crows pierce the quiet.

Peace, rest, hope and promise

Fill the forest with confident expectation.

Joy arises, energy lifts, vision emerges.

Delicious daybreak shines into the future.

Lord, thank You for a fresh start each day. Your mercy is overwhelming. Help me to live in the hope Your compassion brings and pass it onto those around me. In Jesus' merciful name, amen.

Discovery

And God saw everything that He had made, and behold, it was very good (suitable, pleasant) and He approved it completely... Genesis 1:31a AMP

God's wonders never cease to amaze me! Today I discovered a truly wondrous creation in a very small package. As I was walking close to the river, I sat down on a fallen tree to take a rest and soak in the peace and quiet. Out of the corner of my eye, I spotted a slight movement on the tree trunk. When I looked more closely, it appeared to be a traveling cluster of twigs and moss!

My mind was protesting loudly what my eyes were seeing, "Sticks and moss don't crawl!" But this tiny mass of moving plant life was surely making its way down the log. I was totally spellbound. As I moved closer to inspect this little wonder, it stopped and a tiny dark head popped back into one end of the sticks and closed itself up like a turtle escaping into its shell. Amazing!

I never knew this kind of creature existed. It was sort of like a caterpillar in a portable cocoon. I felt like a child again as I pondered this curious little creature. Obviously, he did not share my excitement. His reaction to my presence was instant and he never moved again while I sat there.

After quite a long wait, I finally decided to continue my walk although a bit disappointed that I could not see my discovery in action again. Isn't it funny how a creature just doing what comes naturally could cause such excitement and joy in another creature. The caterpillar was not seeking to make himself known at all. He was just trying to move from one place to another hoping not to be noticed by a predator.

I stand in wonder today as I ponder the diversity of God's creative ability. He is so ingenious and quite humorous in His expressions. What joy our God took in displaying His imagination and just doing what comes naturally for Him!

Lord, help me to express the creativity you have put in my heart as joyously and spontaneously as You. Please help me to just go about my daily activities trusting that You will display, through my life, the awesome diversity of Your creative genius for others to delight in! Amen.

Truth in the Night

And they that be wise shall shine as the brightness of the firmament; and they that turn many to righteousness as the stars forever and ever. Daniel 12:3 KJV

Walking out into the black space

Void of color and shape and light,

Cold night air tightens around me.

Stillness fills my senses with eerie quiet.

Sounds of solitude are deafening.

Groping for a guiding beam

My eyes begin to make adjustment.

Slowly vague shapes appear

And my steps find a dim path

Into the ocean of darkness.

My eyes are slowly drawn upward

On the horizon and I see it.

A tiny sparkle, a faint glimmer

Inviting, leading me forward

Further into the strange and unfamiliar.

Suddenly, the sparkle begins to multiply...

Now two, now three, four and twenty!

No, not twenty but a hundred, a thousand

Oh, so many, so many

I can't begin to count!

One by one they appear higher, higher

Everywhere, big and small, almost minute,

But dazzling and deliciously bright.

They fill the darkness like jewels,

Gems too exquisite to possess.

Now there are more and more,

Too numerous to even consider,

Flowing with silky smoothness,

Forming a mysterious trail across

Depths of darkness and into infinity.

.

Somehow, the air has lost it's chill.

The quiet is not so profound.

Deep foreboding has given way to hope

And new adventure has appeared.

Light once again dispels darkness.

Lord, make me a bright light in the darkness of this world. Help me to let Your light shine through to point the way for others to discover Your greatness and Your goodness. In Jesus Name, amen.

WINTER

Silent Surprise

*The eyes of the Lord are upon even the weakest worship-
pers who love him, those who wait in hope and
expectation for the strong, steady love of God.*
Psalm 33:18 TPT

We drove up to our cabin today with great expectations of seeing some snow showers predicted by the
TV weatherman. Unfortunately, the closer we got up into
the mountains, the clouds began to dissipate and when
we arrived, the sun was shining quite brightly. So, we
unpacked the car and let go of our hopes of seeing snow
for today. The skies certainly did not look promising and
the sun certainly would not allow it to come.

As night began to fall and we finished our sup-
per, the skies were clear and we closed the curtains and
began to relax and watch a movie. We enjoyed our movie and began to get ready for bed. I prepared the coffee
for the morning and cleared away our clutter from the
day.

As I started to bed, I decided to look out and see
if I could see the stars or the moon in the crisp winter
darkness. Gazing at the stars is so delightful here in the
mountains because there are no street lights or glaring
car lights to diminish the sparkle of heavenly lights in
the sky. The stars seem to multiply and grow brilliant the
longer you gaze into the darkness.

Yes, I could see a few stars and even the almost
full moon was shining brilliantly through the trees and
casting deep shadows on the gleaming white forest
floor.....WHAT?

The forest floor is not white!! I turned the deck lights on and there it was...a blanket of fresh fallen snow! Silently it came and covered the earth while we were watching our movie. What a sweet surprise!

The Lord is so dear to us in such surprising ways. Sometimes, even when we have let go of our hope for certain blessings, He will sneak up on us and bring the blessing to us when we least expect it. What a joy He brings to the heart who has let go of an anticipation for good.

I know hope is an integral part of our faith, but the Lord also knows when we are running low on hope and good expectations. He knows us well and is always trying to turn our attention towards His goodness and greatness. Sometimes we give up too quickly, close the curtains on our expectations and miss the silent coming of His sweet surprises!

Lord, help me to recall Your faithfulness and hold onto the expectations for the good things that You promise in Your Word. Teach me steadfast perseverance and grant me tenacious hope. In Jesus name, amen.

Out of Season

...With men [it is] impossible, but not with God;
for all things are possible with God. Mark 10:27 AMP

It's January in Georgia. Today it is 67 degrees, the sun is shining brightly and the jonquils in my yard are blooming! My Carolina jasmine is blooming on the trellis in the garden. The camellias have bloomed almost all winter. What is going on?

We don't always have extremely cold winters here, like in the North, but it is usually cold enough in January for plants to stay dormant and underground. It seems almost like springtime.

But the calendar says it is not. It says it is the season for dormancy, seclusion and warm clothes. It is the time for snow, sleet and cold air. It is the time for reading books, sitting by the fire and doing indoor activities. Maybe not.

Our souls and bodies get accustomed to routine, time tables, schedules and the patterns of living by the seasons of the year. We like the predictable, the familiar and the plans we have created for ourselves. That seems perfectly normal. Doesn't it? Maybe not.

After all, God Himself designed the seasons and the patterns of life, growth and death in each one of them. God designed plants to live within the structures of each season and time period. True enough.

However, I am also realizing that He is the One who reigns over all of creation, and He can change all these familiar things to suit His own timetable of life, growth and death. I think the Lord is speaking to me to be more alert to these outward signs for my own benefit.

Sometimes, I would rather rest and retreat when the Lord is saying, "Forge ahead." Other times I would like to run ahead and be busy because my mind screams, "Hurry up, you are going to get behind!"

I believe the Lord is saying to my heart, "Listen to My quiet voice. I will lead you safely through life putting you in the right place at the right time. I will prepare you for the unexpected and rescue you from the boredom of the familiar. I know when you should work and bloom and when you should be still and rest. I will make you like your jonquils-glorious in the midst of winter." Maybe so!

Lord, You planned the seasons for life and growth for my life. You know when I need to rest and be quiet and when I need to move ahead. You know when it will be time for me to join You face to face. Grace me to hear Your quiet voice and enjoy the journey of joy You have planned for me. Synchronize my movements with Yours. Make me bloom in winter. In Jesus name, amen.

A Familiar Mystery

The voice of the Lord is powerful; the voice of the Lord is full of majesty. Psalm 29:4 AMP

The wind is an interesting facet of creation. It is invisible, mysterious and powerful. You can hear it loudly at times and sometimes it only whispers and can be easily missed altogether. It gently lifts the wings of a bird or a butterfly to amazing heights. It can also carry objects that weigh tons high off the ground as if they were leaves from a tree.

Wind blows from every direction-north, south, east and west. The wind is always blowing somewhere. Every place on earth is affected by the wind. It knows no boundaries and seems to be limitless. It blows up, it blows down and it blows around and around. Wind is strange and familiar all at the same time.

The voice of God is much the same as wind. His words can be very strange at times. His voice can also be a familiar comfort to the one who has taken time to know Him. To me His voice is mostly quiet and gentle and a bit hard to detect at times. He can also speak with an authority that changes my whole direction and focus.

He speaks through really strange things and also through familiar friends and events. His voice changes everything it touches. His voice is powerful, invisible, mysterious and a bit illusive to our human understanding.

This is what He is saying to me about His voice:

"My voice is in you, around you, above you, below you. I speak perpetually, eternally, moment by moment, age to

age. Just stop, be still and know that I AM. Be tuned in, just as you are now, always waiting to hear, slow to speak and quick to answer My call."

Lord, give me the ability to stop, listen and wait for Your voice. I desire to be a ready listener, a slow speaker and a quick responder to Your voice. Thank You for always being available for a conversation. In Jesus name, amen.

Suddenly

Look! I'm sending my messenger on ahead to clear the way for me. Suddenly, out of the blue, the Leader you've been looking for will enter his Temple--yes, the Messenger of the Covenant, the one you've been waiting for. Look! He's on his way! A Message from the mouth of God-of-the-Angel Armies. Malachi 3:1 MSG

It snowed again in Georgia today! The TV weatherman told us it might possibly come around Atlanta, but mostly south of the city--really bizarre. So, the metro schools did not close, but decided to opt for an early out if need be. Unfortunately, that was a bad decision for thousands of people.

I was 40 minutes from home at 12 noon when I left my meeting. Then, around 5:45pm, I pulled into my driveway breathing a sign of relief and a prayer of thanksgiving! What a challenging journey down a regularly traveled road that turned out not to be so regular.

The snow fell suddenly and abundantly creating a 2 inch coat of ice on every street and expressway in most of the state of Georgia. We Southerners are not experts on ice. Four-wheel drive vehicles are scarce, but thank the Lord we just purchased one for me to drive. It did beautifully even on the many back streets I took to avoid the standstill traffic on the main thoroughfares. But most were not so fortunate, including many school buses and lots of big truckers. Thus, the city was in a gridlock that lasted over 24 hours. It was an unbelievable scenario.

What did I learn through this travel trauma? Well, my patience needs work and my confidence in Holy Spirit to lead needs to grow, just for starters. I did lots of praying, worshipping and repenting for getting so frustrated so quickly. Most of us aren't very good at sitting quietly and listening for that still small voice of calm and comfort. But today was one of those days to practice and learn how valuable it is to develop our spiritual ears.

The beauty of the snow we so rarely enjoy here was quickly overcome by the desire to get to my safe, warm home. The winter wonderland was turning into a disaster area in record time. But amidst all the chaos there were such acts of kindness and mercy going on everywhere. People were stopping to help others who were stuck, others were giving rides to those who abandoned their cars. There were thousands of acts of kindness and bravery that shone clearly within all the chaos.

I also discovered that Holy Spirit really did lead me on some unfamiliar paths to make it home as quickly as I did. Many times I thought I wasn't being patient enough to wait in the stalled traffic longer and forged onto the less traveled back roads to escape the wait. But as it turned out, those little side trips got me home much quicker than others who stayed on the familiar routes. So, I learned that sometimes I don't always recognize the leadership of Holy Spirit when He chooses a less travelled road for me to explore.

And most of all, I am seeing that even with the best of predictions and prophetic forecasts, we may find ourselves unprepared for the challenges coming in the days ahead. Am I ready to face those challenges with confidence that Holy Spirit will lead me home safely even in the midst of chaos? He really is an ever-present companion dwelling in the heart of those who love the Lord, and He CAN be trusted.

Oh, Lord, prepare my heart and my mind to receive Your instruction and comfort in the midst of chaos. Thank You for giving me training sessions to learn of You. When I am weak, You are truly strong. Teach me Your ways and show me Your paths for the days ahead. In the precious name of Jesus, amen.

Memories

And now, Lord, what do I wait for and expect?
My hope and expectation are in You. Psalm 39:7 AMP

Tonight I spent time sorting through several packages of snapshots we have taken of special times here at our cabin. I sorted them into years in an attempt to order our experiences with family and friends to place in our memory book. Each picture brought smiles and remembrances of joyous and pleasant times we have had with our loved ones.

The memories also brought tears to my eyes as I realized how wealthy I have become. I don't mean monetarily wealthy, although we lack for nothing. But the richness I speak of is the abundance of love God has bestowed on me through the ones He has placed closet to my heart.

We have certainly had our times of upheaval and heartache over the years, but my God and my Savior has brought us through them all with a continuing sense of hope and joyful anticipation for the future. Everything in our lives is not the way we would want it to be, but as I looked at those pictures I could feel His presence assuring me that He was still in control and not finished with us yet!

I know we are always to look ahead and not look behind in regret or despair, but tonight looking back has caused me to look at the future with fresh hope. My appreciation for the love and patience of God has taken a giant leap forward and my faith in the ultimate prize of His presence is increasing as I write.

God is so good! He is our Father, our Brother, our Comforter, our Friend, our Teacher, our Healer, Deliverer and Savior! He is the fearless Lover of our souls!

Lord, help me be a faithful lover of the souls you have brought into my life. Thank You for giving me Your extravagant love to share with others and increased hope for the future. In the precious name of Jesus, amen.

Another Log

Generation after generation will declare more of your
greatness, and discover more of your glory...
Psalm 145:4 TPT

Tonight, as I sat alone beside the fireplace reading, I let the fire dwindle down to almost nothing. There
were two logs still on the grate, but the flames had di-
minished considerably. One of the logs had been
reduced to just a row of slow burning coals. The other
one was still recognizable but quite charred and barely
smoldering. The room had grown cold, so I grabbed a
fresh log from the stack beside the hearth to add to the
ones on the grate.

I nestled the new log in between the older ones.
The smoldering log supported the new one and the old
row of coals beneath the two ignited them both. Within a
moment the fire had revived and the heat began to radi-
ate once again from the fireplace warming the air. The
flames quickly increased until there was a roaring fire
glowing in the dim room bringing light and heat to comfort my body and soul.

Gazing into the flames, I was amazed at how
quickly the older logs caught fire as the new log was
added to the pile. By themselves they had lost their energy and almost died out, but the addition of the fresh
log somehow revived them. Together all three burned
passionately creating a beautiful sight.

This phenomenon reminded me of the generations in our families and the Church. When a new
generation arrives and gets almost grown, they tend to
congregate in a group with those their age, wandering
through life without much purpose. They don't spend as

much time with the older generations of parents and grandparents. The middle-aged group gets weighed down with work and responsibility and tends to forget how to enjoy life. The older generation seems to smolder alone just remembering the heat of their younger years rather than experiencing the joy of their remaining days on earth.

However, when the generations come together in true relationship, the atmosphere changes rapidly. The young ones add needed energy to the air and the middle age group steps up to the plate with financial and emotional support to guide the way. The older ones add their experience and memories of past victories and lessons learned in failure.

Together the fire once again bursts forth, lives are filled with warmth and light is seen again in the eyes of each generation. God's family plan is never obsolete!

Lord, I pray that You will be known and worshipped in all my generations on this earth now and in the future. May Your glorious works be remembered and preserved through the generations of my family and Your church for the glory of Jesus' name. Amen.

ABOUT THE AUTHOR

Angela Brown is a student and lover of the Word of God. She loves interceding in prayer and sharing her faith through writing and speaking. She is the best-selling author of *Prayers that Avail Much for Children,* a prayer book based on Scripture created for young children. She is also the author of *His Footstool: The Door to Your Destiny,* a study of Psalm 110, suitable for individual and group studies.

Angela has written articles for periodicals and assisted other authors in compiling and writing their own publications. She enjoys being an active intercessor with the Word of Love ministry for over 25 years. One of her joys is teaching the Word of God and encouraging others to thrive in their creative gifting. She is also the founder of Dream Gate Publishing.

Angela and her husband, Jackie, have been married 48 years and reside in Marietta, Georgia close to their children, grandchildren and great grandchildren.

Made in the USA
Charleston, SC
31 December 2016